Core
training

Core
training

Sara Rose

This is a Parragon Publishing Book
First published in 2006

Parragon Publishing
Queen Street House
4 Queen Street
Bath BA1 1HE, UK

ISBN: 1-40548-629-5
Printed in China

Created and produced by the Bridgewater Book Company Ltd
Photography: Ian Parsons
Hair and make-up: Sarah Jane Froom and Tracy Swan
Models: Charlotte Curtis and Scott Virgo

▼ # contents

There are many approaches to improving your fitness, but one of the most popular over the past few years has been that of improving your core stability. The "core" of the body is simply what's between the shoulders and hips—basically, the trunk and pelvis. Draw an imaginary line around the center of your body, starting at your navel, and most of the muscles bordering that line are your core muscles. This book is a guide to the safe and effective training of these core muscles, which are vital for a healthy back and a key component of fitness.

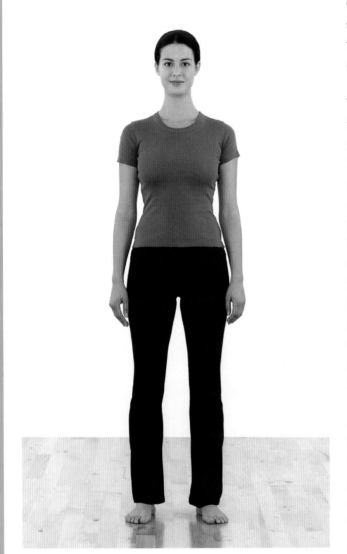

Core training is a system that re-educates your body so that you use it effectively. It's an intelligent workout that strengthens your body from the inside out and is a safe and effective way to exercise.

The core is a crucial group of muscles, not only for sports, but for typical daily activities as well. It's essential that your core is strong because it comes into play just about every time you move. The core acts to produce force (for example, lifting), it stabilizes the body to permit other musculature to produce force (for example, during running), and it's also called upon to transfer energy (for example, during jumping). Everyone can benefit from core training, from new exercisers working on their fitness to exercise enthusiasts looking for increased performance. It can help the elderly who wish to remain fit and flexible, and women after pregnancy to get their abdominal and pelvic floor muscles back into shape.

A well-developed core region will act as a solid block on which the chest cavity sits, preventing it from moving during strenuous lifting exercises. Most gym-goers do a few crunches and the odd rowing exercise, but their goal is usually aesthetic. Training for the perfect set of abs (also known as the "six-pack") and core training are different. Looking good

◉ introduction

when your stomach's on display is one thing, but being able to avoid lower-back problems and injuries is more important.

Core training will also tone your torso and abdominal muscles and improve your posture—if your core is strong, your lower abdominal muscles will be drawn in toward the spine and help you sit up straight. Your balance and coordination will be improved, and, most important of all, core stability will help keep your spine healthy and flexible throughout life.

How to use this book

Read through the introductory pages before trying the exercises so that you understand vital safety points and how to perform the exercises correctly. Follow the exercise planners for guidance on how to put an exercise routine together, but remember not to do too many exercises at once. Carry out core training exercises at least three times a week if you can and build up the amount of time you spend on each exercise and the types of exercise that you do.

1

THE BASICS

This chapter is an introduction to the mechanics of your body's core. There are sound anatomical reasons for core strengthening, which are easy to appreciate once you understand the relationship between the stomach muscles and the spine. There's also a section on posture, which has a crucial part to play in core training. Plus, you'll find information on what you need to do before you get started—safety tips, choosing the right equipment, and creating the right environment so you can exercise safely.

Core stability is the effective use of the core muscles to help stabilize the spine, allowing your limbs to move more freely. Good core stability means you can keep your midsection rigid without forces such as gravity affecting your movements. The positive effects of this include reducing the likelihood of injury, better posture, increased agility and flexibility, and improved coordination. Core training also helps to improve your proprioception—the way your body reacts and recovers from being unbalanced.

Core training aims to increase your core stability by developing trunk fitness, which is relevant to everyday life rather than just to sport. How often do you find yourself in an everyday situation that requires you to do one hundred sit-ups? Not very often, but when you are reaching to pick up a child, for example, you require a fundamental core strength in order not only to pick up the child but also to avoid injuring yourself.

There are many ways of improving core stability, from traditional abdominal exercises to movement therapies such as pilates and yoga and even water-based exercise. To really capture the benefits of core strength, including better alignment, balance, and functional movement (as well as flat abs), it is necessary to work the deep, underlying abdominal and back musculature.

One way to make sure that you are targeting these deep muscles is to get off solid ground and onto an unstable surface, such as an exercise ball or a wobble board. The instability created by these pieces of equipment forces you to adopt the correct posture in preparation for and during exercises, and maintaining that posture engages the deep muscles. When you add exercise on top of that, it's a powerhouse combination to strengthen your core. Using a ball or a wobble board may be difficult for beginners, so progress to this stage at your own pace.

▼ what is core stability?

How to train your core

Traditional abdominal training can be boring to many people. Endless crunches are not only monotonous, but also ineffective because they don't target the deep muscles. The abdominals are muscles just like any other and should be trained using the same principles as any other muscle group. They should be loaded with resistance, and challenged in a variety of ways—by lateral (side) flexion, bending forward and backward, and rotation. If strength and muscle development is the goal, hundreds of repetitions are not necessary. Core strength should be developed gradually, to decrease the risk of injury. When starting out on a core training program, you need to progress properly:

• Start with the easiest movements and progress to more difficult movements.

• Initially, you may not require any extra load but, as you adapt, you can increase the resistance by using weights, changing the position, etc.

• Perform all movements in a slow and controlled manner until coordination, strength, and confidence permit higher-speed movements.

• To increase the complexity and muscle demands of the exercises, many moves can be performed lying prone (face down) or supine (on your back) on an exercise ball or other unstable platform after you have mastered them on the floor.

The spine (backbone) is an S-shaped, flexible curve that is key to how the different parts of your body interact. It supports your skull, acts as a structural base for your limbs, ribs, and pelvis to attach to, and enables you to stand upright. The spine (along with the ribs) protects the internal organs, and encases the spinal cord (which carries messages between the brain and the spinal nerves). It also provides movement for your trunk, letting you twist and bend forward, backward, and to the side.

The spine comprises 33 vertebrae (bones) stacked on top of one another and linked by bony projections called facet joints, which enable the vertebrae to move. Each vertebra is separated from the next by a disk, which acts as a cushion or shock absorber. Each disk has a hard outer casing and a spongy center, which is kept healthy through movement. As the spine moves, fluids are pressed in and waste products squeezed out. The vertebrae are connected by several layers of muscles that criss-cross from vertebra to vertebra, up and down the spine, to hold it together. The spinal bones are divided into five groups (cervical, thoracic, lumbar, sacrum, and coccyx). In this book we are most concerned with the lumbar vertebrae, the large, strong bones in the lower spine that are covered with powerful muscles and permit flexion and extension.

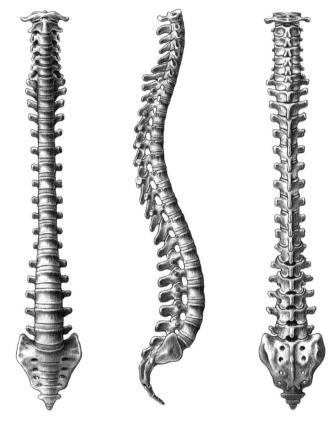

The spine has three natural curves: in at the back of the neck, outward at the back of the rib cage and in again in the lower back (lumbar spine). The function of these spinal curves is to absorb some of the shock of movement and make actions more agile. Poor posture and long periods spent sitting down will alter the position of the spinal curves, resulting in back pain. To protect your spine, you should aim to maintain its natural curve to minimize the stress put upon the ligaments and disks, particularly in the lumbar region. This is called putting your spine into neutral, and nearly every exercise in this book will require you to do this. It's essential that you can perform this maneuver correctly in order for the exercises to be effective, so use the following instructions as a guide:

▼ all about the spine

Standing neutral

1 Stand tall against a wall with your buttocks and shoulders touching the wall. Keep your feet parallel and hip-width apart, with your weight evenly dispersed on both feet. Gently pull up through your legs, keeping your knees slightly bent, and pull your tailbone down toward the floor.

2 Place one hand between the wall and your lower back. The neutral position is slightly different for everyone, but it should feel comfortable and you should just be able to place the flat of your hand between your back and the wall. If you can get only your fingers through, your back is too flat and your pelvis is tilted too far forward. If you can get your whole hand through, then your back is too arched and your pelvis too far back.

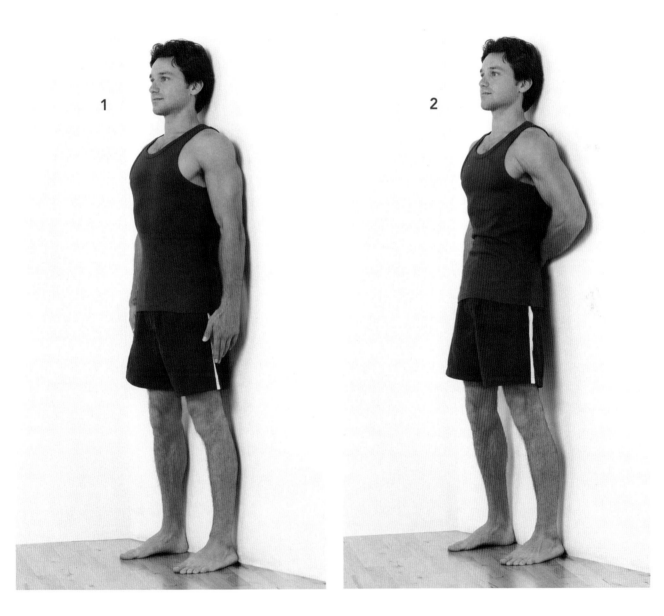

1

2

Lying down neutral

1 Lie down on your back with your knees bent and your feet flat on the floor, hip-width apart. Your spine will be flat against the floor, apart from the curve of the neck and the lower back.

2 Press your waist back onto the floor by tilting your pelvis back so that you lose the curve in your lower back. Now tilt your pelvis forward so that your lower back overarches. Then find the midpoint between these two extremes. You should be able to slip one hand under your waist and feel a slight gap between your waist and the floor.

2

Sitting neutral

1 Sit up straight on a stool or chair with your weight evenly distributed on both buttocks. Place your feet flat on the floor, hip-width apart.

2 Look straight ahead and keep your spine and neck long. Pull your shoulder blades down toward your waist to stop your shoulders from hunching.

3 The natural curves at your neck and your waist should be evident.

Variation

Sit tall on an exercise ball with your back straight and both feet flat on the floor, hip-width apart. Gently squeeze your shoulder blades together to stop them from rounding. Tilt your pelvis forward to increase the curve in the lumbar spine, trying to pull your buttocks upward. Then tilt the pelvis backward to flatten the curve in your lower spine. After finding the two extremes of movement, reduce the tilting until you are about midway between the two. This neutral position should feel comfortable.

PROTECTING YOUR SPINE WHILE EXERCISING

• Be conscious of your neck—it's fine to cradle the sides of your head with your hands, but avoid resting your head on your hands because you may pull on your neck.
• Keep your abdominal muscles pulled in—this will protect your lower spine.
• Exercise on a mat or other padded surface to prevent bruising.
• Always keep your knees slightly bent when performing leg exercises—straight-leg exercising makes your hip flexors pull directly on the spine, causing excessive stress on your lower back.

Posture refers to the alignment of your muscles and joints. Good posture happens when your spine is in its natural alignment and permits normal movement without discomfort or pain. It helps you stand and sit properly, reduces the strain on your back, and allows your internal organs to function efficiently.

An automatic mechanism in your brain controls your posture and responds to feedback from messages sent by your muscles. For example, if you lean to the left side, your brain will send messages to muscles on your right side to contract in order to correct this movement and restore your balance. If your posture is consistently poor over a period of time, your muscles will be subjected to uneven stresses, leading to aching muscles and joints, tiredness, weakness, and an increased risk of injury when exercising. Causes of poor posture include: being overweight, pregnancy, foot problems and wearing ill-fitting footwear, weak muscles, and injuries.

Good posture looks natural and relaxed, not slouched and hunched. When you are standing up, your neck should be in line with your spine, with your head balanced squarely on top, your shoulder blades set back and down, and your spine long and curving naturally. Your hips should be straight. Good posture when sitting means sitting up straight with your feet flat on the floor and your lower back supported.

How to check your posture

Stand tall in front of a full-length mirror to assess your posture when you are standing. Check to see whether the following applies:

- Ear lobes level
- Shoulders level
- Equal distance between shoulders and ears
- Equal distance between arms and body
- Hips level
- Kneecaps level

Now turn and look at yourself sideways. Imagine there is a straight line drawn down the center of your body. If your posture is spot-on, the line will pass through the center of the ear lobe, the tip of the shoulder, halfway through the chest, slightly behind the hip, and just outside the ankle bone.

It does take time to correct any postural deficiencies you may have but it is important to identify what your weaknesses are—for example, rounded shoulders —so that you can work on correcting these. The good news is that by training your core muscles you will be strengthening the muscles that hold up your back and automatically improving your posture.

▼ posture

TIPS FOR IMPROVING POSTURE

• Sleep on your back rather than on your front.

• Keep your head up and your shoulders back when walking.

• Bend your knees rather than your back when bending over to pick something up.

• Brace your abdominal muscles before lifting a heavy object; bend your knees rather than your back to pick it up and then carry it close to your body.

• If you tend to carry a lot in your shoulder bag or briefcase, you'd be better off using a rucksack to disperse the weight evenly.

Muscles are made up of millions of tiny protein filaments that contract and relax to produce movement. Most muscles are attached to bones by tendons and are controlled by your brain. Nerves transmit electrical messages from the brain, which cause the cells within the muscles to contract. Movement is caused by muscles pulling on tendons, which move the bones at the joints. Muscles work in pairs so that bones can move in two directions, and most movements involve the use of several muscle groups. Anterior muscles are in the front of the body, posterior muscles at the back.

The muscles you need to know about in order to improve your core stability are those that are arranged around your torso. At the front and side are the four main abdominal muscles, at the back are the spinal extensors and multifidus, and at the base of the trunk are the pelvic floor muscles.

Abdominal muscles

The abdominal muscles form a natural corset around your middle. They support the spine, protect internal organs, and enable you to sit, twist, and bend. The rectus abdominis is the muscle that runs from the bottom of your ribs to the pubic bone. When highly toned, it creates the "six-pack" look, but its actual purpose is to let you bend forward and sit up from a lying position. At the side of the torso are two diagonal muscles: the internal oblique and the external oblique. These bend the spine to the side and rotate it. Underneath the obliques lies the transversus abdominis, the deepest layer of muscles in your core, which wraps horizontally around your torso like a corset from the rib cage to the pubic bone until it merges with the sheath covering the rectus abdominis. The transversus abdominis is responsible for trunk stability and pulls your stomach in tight.

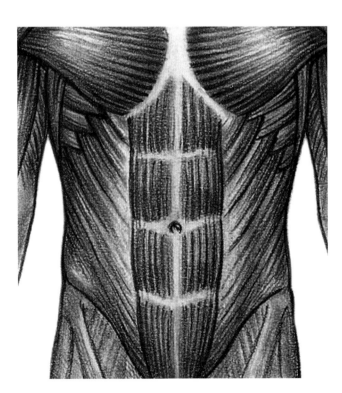

▼ core muscles

Back muscles

There are two groups of back muscles (spinal extensors) that are important to core stability. The first group attach between each of the vertebrae; the second attach along the whole length of the spine. The multifidus is the most important of these muscles because it stiffens the spine and can also flatten the lumbar curve without moving the whole spine.

Pelvic floor muscles

These attach to the inside of the pelvis, forming a sling from the tailbone at the back to the pubic bone at the front. The pelvic floor muscles are vital for continence and help to maintain intra-abdominal pressure, which is important for stabilization.

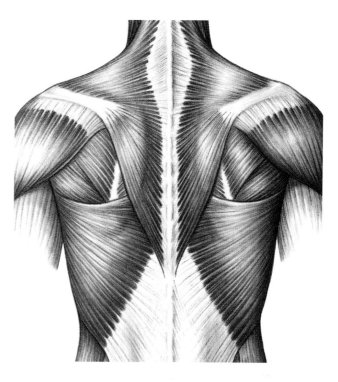

PELVIC FLOOR CONTRACTIONS

It's just as important for men to keep their pelvic floor muscles in good trim to prevent incontinence as it is for women. Lie on your back with your knees bent and your feet slightly apart, flat on the floor. Relax your buttock muscles. Slowly tighten your pelvic floor muscles as if you were trying to stop passing water midstream, and try not to tense your buttock muscles. Hold for a count of 5 then release.

Trunk muscles

The trunk muscles fall into two categories: inner (primarily responsible for stabilization) and outer (mainly responsible for movement). The inner unit muscles include the transversus abdominis (which plays the major part), diaphragm, multifidus, and pelvic floor; the outer unit includes the obliques and spinal erectors. The inner and outer units work together to create spinal stability and enable subsequent movement.

Setting your abdominal muscles

This procedure is known as abdominal hollowing, setting, or bracing and involves tightening the transversus abdominis so that it maintains stability of the spine while you are exercising. Doing this correctly is vital for successful core training, and the following exercises demonstrate abdominal setting in the key positions required for core training exercises, namely standing, kneeling, sitting, and lying.

Standing abdominal hollowing

1 Stand upright with your feet hip-width apart. Keep your spine in neutral.

2 Focus on your navel and draw it in by tightening your muscles, not by sucking in your waist or holding your breath. Restrict the movement to your stomach muscles; do not tilt your pelvis or flatten your back.

Kneeling abdominal hollowing

1 Position yourself on all fours (the "box" position) with your hands and knees shoulder-width apart.

2 Let your stomach muscles relax and sag downward, then tighten them and pull them up and in. The amount of movement may be very small to begin with but should increase to about 4 in (10 cm) with practice. Don't arch your back or tilt your pelvis—the movement should be restricted to the stomach area.

2

Prone abdominal hollowing

1 Lie face down on the floor with your arms by your sides, palms up. Place a cushion beneath your forehead for comfort.

2 Pull your navel up and inward and draw your abdominal wall off the floor, but don't lift your chest. If you have excess weight on your stomach you may not be able to do this.

Sitting abdominal hollowing

1 Sit on a stool or exercise ball with your feet apart.

2 Sit up straight and place one hand on your stomach, the other in the small of your back—this will help you to monitor the position of your spine. Pull your navel in and up away from your front hand.

TIP

Breathe normally when practicing abdominal hollowing; do not take a deep breath when trying to flatten your stomach. If your rib cage rises during the movement, you have taken a deep breath.

A little preparation goes a long way when it comes to exercising. In the following pages you'll find useful tips on what equipment you will need, what to wear, when and where to exercise, and how to breathe effectively to make the most of your workout.

Equipment

The amount of equipment you need is up to you —there are plenty of pieces of equipment that create an unstable base and make your core muscles work really hard. These range from wobble boards to medicine balls, exercise balls, resistance bands, and even adjustable cable pulley machines if you're in the gym. For the purpose of this book we recommend an exercise ball and/or a wobble board for variation. Hand weights and ankle weights can be used (but not if you're new to exercise or have back problems) —make sure they are not too heavy. Small cushions or folded towels make ideal padding during exercises which involve lying on the floor or kneeling.

exercise ball

wobble board

resistance band

gym mat

ankle weights

before you begin

What to wear

Avoid wearing clothing that will restrict your movements and choose clothes in which you can exercise comfortably, such as a T-shirt and leggings/tracksuit pants or shorts. Cotton and natural fibers are cooler than manmade ones, and it's best to wear layers that you can remove as necessary. Wear sneakers or exercise in bare feet—don't work out in socks because you might slip. Remove jewelry and belts, and tie your hair back if it is long.

Environment

Find a quiet, comfortable, clutter-free space to work out in. You need a nonslip surface such as an exercise mat or a carpet to protect your spine and prevent bruising. If possible, try to exercise in front of a full-length mirror so that you can check what you are doing.

When to exercise

You need to wait at least an hour after eating before exercising, but otherwise you can perform these exercises at any time of the day. Choose the time that suits you best, whether it's a morning session to give you a burst of energy at the start of the day or an evening one to help you unwind after a busy day. But don't exercise immediately before going to bed because you'll find it difficult to get to sleep.

How many exercises?

It's the quality of the movement that counts, so start gently and build up the number of repetitions as you become fitter. Don't attempt to do too much too soon. In general you should aim for one set (usually 6–8 repetitions) of each exercise before moving on to the next one.

Concentration and focus

To get the most benefit from each exercise, you need to concentrate on how and where you are moving. By doing this you are more likely to move correctly and safely. This will also help you to interpret the way your body responds to each move and judge more accurately the correct state of tension or relaxation that is required. Use positive thoughts while you are exercising and focus on what you are doing right. Telling yourself that you are doing well can make you do even better.

Breathing

Breathing is something we all do without thinking but it can be consciously controlled. Correct breathing comes from the deepest area of the lungs, but most of us have shallow, rapid breathing and use only the top third of the lungs. Breathing properly encourages effective oxygenation of the blood, allowing muscles and organs to work efficiently. It also relaxes muscles and releases tension and enables you to contract your inner unit properly. You need to practice abdominal, or diaphragmatic, breathing, which allows the lungs to fill and empty with minimal effort. This will make your exercising much more effective—though you will find it quite difficult to do at first.

1 Sit in a comfortable position with your back supported. Place one hand on your chest and the other on your abdomen just below the breastbone. If the hand on your chest moves more than the one on your abdomen as you breathe, then your breathing is mainly in the upper chest. Try to breathe so that only your lower hand is moving.

2 Now place both hands on your abdomen just below the ribs. Breathe in slowly through your nose. Pause for a few seconds then breathe out through your mouth, letting out as much air as possible, feeling your abdomen fall as your diaphragm relaxes.

3 Repeat 3 or 4 times.

1

2

2

WARMING UP

Before embarking on an exercise routine to train your core muscles, it is important to warm up the specific muscles and joints that you will be using in order to prevent injury. A warm-up should replicate the movements you are about to do but should graduate in intensity and range to mobilize the relevant muscles and joints in all directions. The following exercises will warm up your core muscles and also mobilize your hips, spine, and shoulders. You don't need any specialist equipment to perform these exercises but it is important to do them properly and not rush them. The emphasis is on slow, controlled movements that prepare your body for activity.

Standing Pelvic Tilt

Pelvic tilting teaches you how to control the lumbar spine during exercise. The aim here is to practice finding your neutral spine position as this is essential for performing core stability exercises successfully. The action should be confined to your lower back—avoid any body sway. You may find that, to begin with, placing your hands either side of your waist will help you to stay balanced and correct any swaying.

1 Stand tall against a wall with your feet hip-width apart, arms by your sides.

2 Tilt your hips back and forth a few times—when tilting your pelvis forward you should be able to fit one hand into the gap between your lower back and the wall as your lower back hollows. When you tilt your pelvis backward you should feel your lower back press against your hand as it flattens. Aim to find the midrange of this spinal movement, between the two extremes—this is your neutral spine position.

2

Standing Abdominal Hollowing

For all the core stability exercises you have to activate the deep inner-unit muscles in a hollowing action; therefore the abdominal hollowing exercise (also known as setting or bracing) that rehearses this action is essential as part of your warm-up. The action itself should feel light and subtle—do not hold your breath or suck in your waist because you won't be using your deep stabilizing muscles. Keep your hips, legs, and spine still and restrict movement to your stomach muscles alone—try not to tilt your pelvis or flatten your back.

1 Stand tall with your feet hip-width apart and your spine in neutral.

2 Pull your stomach muscles in and up to hollow your abdomen, keeping your attention focused on your navel. Imagine that there is a belt around your waist and that you are simply tightening the belt one notch. Hold for a count of 5.

3 Perform 3 repetitions.

2

CAUTION
Always check with your doctor before embarking on an exercise routine—this is essential if you have ever had any back problems.

Full Body Reach-Up

This opens and strengthens your shoulders, lengthens your spine and neck, and improves your posture. Keep your arms straight throughout the exercise.

1

2

1 Stand with your feet close together, knees soft, spine in neutral, and abdominal muscles set.

2 Slowly raise your arms up from each side, bringing your palms together above your head.

3 Take your arms back down to the starting position.

4 Perform 4 repetitions.

Torso Rotations

Gradually increase the range of movement as you do this exercise, reaching across your torso with your opposite hand as you do so. The twisting action should force you to come up on to the toes of your opposite foot.

2

1 Keep your pelvis in neutral and stand with your feet hip-width apart and knees slightly bent.

2 Rotate your torso to one side then the other, increasing the range of movement as you do so. You should feel a slight stretch across your back and shoulders.

3 Perform 5–10 repetitions.

Side Bends

Keep your pelvis in neutral throughout and be careful to avoid leaning forward or backward while doing this exercise.

1 Stand with your feet hip-width apart, knees slightly bent, and arms by your side.

2 Bend sideways at the waist and extend your left hand down your left leg, then stand up straight again.

2

1

3 Repeat on your right side. Bend a little further as you repeat the exercise, making sure you do not twist or bend your spine as you do so.

4 Perform 5–10 repetitions.

CONTROLLING YOUR MOVEMENTS

Each movement should flow in a gentle, slow manner to let your muscles warm up and stretch naturally. Think about what you're doing and try to keep your body relaxed as you move. Never stretch further than is comfortable or bounce into position. If any action hurts, you're not doing it properly.

Spinal Curl

This exercise will create flexibility and strength in your spine and relax your shoulders.

1 Stand with your feet hip-width apart and your knees "soft" (slightly bent). Bend your knees and put your hands on your thighs, just above the knees.

2 Push your buttocks away and let your lower spine curl downward, making a concave shape.

3 Now, tightening your abdominal muscles, arch your lower back upward, then release back to the concave shape.

4 Perform 5–10 repetitions, increasing the movement with each repetition.

2

Marching on the Spot

This exercise increases hip and knee flexibility, strengthens hip flexor muscles, raises your pulse rate and body temperature, and improves coordination between the right and left sides of your body.

1 Stand with your feet hip-width apart, your spine in neutral, and your abdominal muscles braced to begin. Look straight ahead.

2 March on the spot for about a minute, lifting your knees as high as is comfortable and swinging each arm in turn toward your opposite knee as you march.

3

STANDING AND SITTING EXERCISES

In this section you will find basic standing and sitting exercises to improve core stability. Many are traditional abdominal exercises or established moves from exercise systems such as yoga and pilates and have varying degrees of difficulty. Some exercises incorporate the use of an unstable surface, such as a wobble board (which at its most basic is a board on top of half a ball) or an exercise ball, which forces you to activate your inner unit for balancing, and is thus extremely effective at training core stability.

Roll Down the Wall

This is a great warm-up exercise for your back. The aim is to lengthen the spine and increase its flexibility, strengthen your abdominal muscles, and help build core strength. Keep your breathing controlled and regular throughout.

1 Stand about 1 ft (30 cm) away from a wall with your feet parallel and hip-width apart, and your knees slightly bent. Lean back on the wall to support your spine. Put your pelvis in neutral and tighten your abdominal muscles.

2 Slowly roll down off the wall by dropping your chin toward your chest and letting the weight of your head draw you downward, trying to avoid swaying from side to side. Let your arms dangle down.

3 Roll down as far as is comfortable (ideally, until your hands touch the floor) then reverse the motion so that you come back up to a standing position.

4 Perform 5 repetitions.

1

Standing Forward Bend

This stretches and strengthens your spine, helps you to stand properly, and helps build core strength.

CAUTION
Both these exercises involve forward flexion (bending) of the spine, and you should consult your doctor before doing them if you have a history of lower-back problems.

1 Stand up straight with your spine in neutral and your feet close together, knees slightly bent, and your arms by your side. Set your abdominal muscles.

2 Bend forward until your body is at a 90-degree angle and your hands are behind you.

3 Return to the start position.

4 Perform 5 repetitions.

2

Standing on One Leg

This exercise will improve your proprioception—your perception of the relative position and movement of the different parts of your body. To make it more difficult, close your eyes during this exercise.

1 Stand up straight with your knees "soft" (slightly bent) and feet together. Keep your spine in neutral and set your abdominals. Place your weight on your right leg. You may raise your arms in front of you to help you keep your balance.

2 Lift your left foot no more than 2 in (5 cm) off the ground and hold for 15 seconds.

3 Repeat on the other leg.

4 Perform 4–6 repetitions.

Horizontal Balance

The aim in this exercise is to keep your balance with minimal movement—avoid tilting your pelvis as you bend forward.

1 Stand up straight with your knees slightly bent and your spine in neutral. Tighten your abdominal muscles.

2 Transfer your weight onto one leg and bend at the hip so that you lean forward, extending the other leg behind you as you bend and extending your arms forward.

3 Lean forward as far as possible or until you are horizontal. Hold for a count of 5 then return to the starting position.

4 Repeat on the other leg.

2

T'AI CHI

There are many forms of exercise and movement therapies that will help to improve core stability. T'ai Chi, a noncombative martial art, is very useful for core training because of its emphasis on balance and good posture.

3

Standing Leg Lift

This will help improve your balance, stabilize the pelvis, and tone your thigh and hip muscles. Aim to keep your pelvis stable throughout.

1 Stand with your spine in neutral, feet slightly apart, and arms by your sides.

2 Pull your navel in toward your spine and bring your left knee in toward your chest so that your big toe is resting on the side of your right knee. Hold your knee with both hands, keeping your spine straight and your standing leg strong. You will need to drop your left hip down and lift the hip higher on the right side to keep your hips level at this point.

2

4

3 Hold for a count of 3 then release.

4 Repeat with the other leg.

5 Perform 4–6 repetitions.

Variation

To make this exercise more difficult, after step 2 stretch your left leg straight out in front of you at hip height, holding on to the back of your thigh to support it. Release your arms and rest them on your buttocks, but keep your left leg extended in front of you. Hold for up to 10 seconds then lower your leg to the floor and repeat on the other leg. Perform 4–6 repetitions on each leg.

Side Standing Leg Lift

This works your abdominal muscles and back extensors as well as your quadriceps, hamstrings, and gluteals (buttock muscles).

1 Stand up straight with your spine in neutral, your feet hip-width apart, and arms by your sides. Set your abdominal muscles.

2 Support your body weight on your right leg and lift your left leg to the side. As you do this extend your right arm forward and your left arm out to the side. Hold for a count of 3.

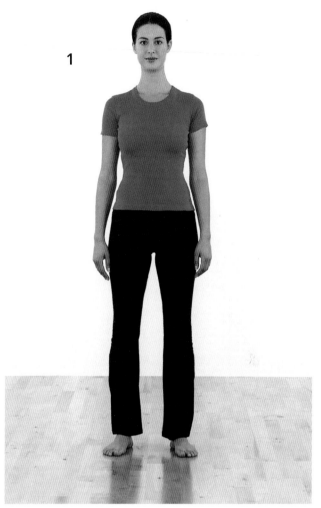

3 Repeat on the other side.

4 Perform 6–8 repetitions.

TIP
Add ankle weights for an increased challenge—but only when you can perform the leg lifts perfectly.

Lunge

The farther you step forward in this exercise, the harder your muscles will be worked.

1 Stand with your hands on your hips and your feet parallel and hip-width apart. Brace your abdominal muscles.

2 Take a big step forward, keeping your weight evenly balanced between both legs.

3 Bend both knees as far as is comfortable so that you lower your torso down, then return to the starting position.

4 Repeat on the other leg.

5 Perform 6–8 repetitions.

Basic Squat

Keep your spine in neutral and do not allow your pelvis to tilt as you squat down.

1 Start by standing in a level position with your feet parallel and wide apart and your hands on your hips. Keep your spine in neutral alignment and tighten your abdominal muscles. Bend your knees as if you're about to sit down.

2 Squat down as far as you can without losing your balance or arching your back.

3 Hold for a count of 1, then push through your heels to return to the starting position.

4 Perform 6–8 repetitions.

Squat with Leg Lift

This move works your entire lower body. Focus on keeping your abdominal muscles braced to maintain your balance.

1 Stand on the floor with your feet parallel and hip-width apart. Place your hands on your hips, set your abdominal muscles, and bend your knees so that you squat.

2 Press up into a standing position as you simultaneously extend your right leg to the side.

3 Return to the squatting position.

4 Repeat on the other side.

5 Perform 6–8 repetitions.

Standing Circle

This exercise stretches and strengthens the sides of your back and abdomen. The movement should come from your upper body rather than your hips.

1 Stand up with your spine in neutral and your feet hip-width apart, knees slightly bent. Raise your arms and hold a small towel or resistance band taut over your head.

2

1

2 Tighten your abdominal muscles and slowly draw a circle over your head and around your torso with your hands, keeping the towel pulled taut throughout.

3 Return to the starting position and reverse the circular movement.

4 Perform 6–8 repetitions in each direction.

Seated Forward Spine Stretch

This exercise helps you to sit with good posture because it strengthens your transversus abdominis. Make sure you don't hunch your shoulders.

1 Sit on the floor with your legs extended in front of you, knees slightly bent, and feet flexed. Set your abdominal muscles and extend your arms in front of you at chest level.

2 Curl your body forward, keeping your abdominal muscles pulled back in toward your spine.

3 Roll back to the starting position, using your abdominal muscles to pull yourself up.

4 Perform 4 repetitions.

1

TIP
Remember—it's the quality of movement that counts rather than the number of repetitions.

2

Seated Leg Lift

Sitting on an exercise ball and lifting your feet from the floor is a great way to train your core muscles. This exercise challenges your balance and helps you control movement of the pelvis. It's important to use your core muscles to keep your pelvis stable throughout the exercise.

1 Sit up straight on an exercise ball with your spine in neutral. Raise your arms out to your sides at shoulder height to help you balance and tighten your abdominal muscles to support your lower back. Your feet should be on the floor, parallel, and hip-width apart.

2 Keeping your knee bent, lift your right leg about 4 in (10 cm) off the floor and hold for a count of 10, making sure you don't arch your back as you do so. Don't lift your feet too high or you will wobble and lose your postural alignment.

3 Repeat on the left leg.

4 Perform 3–5 repetitions.

TIP
To make the exercise harder, lift both feet off the floor at the same time.

2

Seated Pelvic Tilt

Try to keep your upper body relatively still as you perform this exercise. You can increase the size of the movements to make your abdominal muscles work even harder to maintain your balance.

1 Sit with good posture on an exercise ball with your spine in neutral and your feet shoulder-width apart. Keep your arms by your sides or fold them in front of you at shoulder height.

2 Set your abdominal muscles by gently pulling your navel in toward your spine.

3 Gently tilt your pelvis backward and forward using very small movements so that you are slightly increasing the curve in your back then flattening it.

4 Perform 10–15 repetitions.

1

3

Seated Spinal Twist

This exercise works your obliques. Aim to keep your spine straight without rounding your back.

1 Sit up straight with your legs extended in front of you, knees slightly bent, and feet flexed. Raise your arms to the sides at shoulder height and tighten your abdominal muscles to support your back.

2 Turn your head and shoulders toward your left, keeping your back, hips, and buttocks motionless as you move.

3 Rotate as far as is comfortable then hold for a count of 1. Return to the starting position and repeat on the other side.

4 Perform 6–8 repetitions on each side, rotating a little farther the easier it becomes.

1

Variation

Sitting on an exercise ball while doing spinal twists further challenges your core muscles. Keep your knees still during this exercise—if they do move, this shows that your pelvis is not stable.

3

Mermaid

This exercise works your obliques and increases lateral flexion. Try to keep your spine straight and do not lean forward or backward. If you don't have an exercise ball, you can kneel with your feet under your buttocks instead.

ALEXANDER TECHNIQUE
This is a method that aims to improve posture so that your body operates with minimum strain. Students relearn basic movements such as sitting and standing and how to align the body so they can move in a relaxed, fluid way.

2

1 Sit up on the ball with good posture, your spine in neutral, and your feet parallel on the floor and hip-width apart. Tighten your abdominal muscles and let your arms rest by your sides.

2 Reach your right arm up to the ceiling and lean over to the left side so that you reach the right arm over your head. Hold for a count of 1 then lower your arm.

3 Repeat on the other side.

4 Perform 3 repetitions.

Seated Reverse Abdominal Curl

This is an easy exercise that can be done almost anywhere. It works your rectus abdominis. Try to avoid sagging or arching the back and hold your abdominal muscles in tight throughout the movement.

1 Sit on a stool or on a bench with your spine in neutral. Set your abdominal muscles and extend your arms in front of you at shoulder height.

2 Slowly lean your torso and shoulders backward, keeping the spine rigid, as far back as is comfortable.

3 Hold the position for a count of 2 then return to the starting position.

4 Perform 6–8 repetitions.

1

2

Seated Lateral Curl

This is quite a challenging exercise and should be attempted only when you are confident that you can easily maintain your balance on an exercise ball. It gives all your abdominal muscles a good workout. To increase the stabilization control required, bring your feet closer together at the start.

1 Sit on the ball with your spine in neutral, your feet hip-width apart. Set your abdominal muscles and roll forward with your pelvis until the ball is under your lower spine.

2 Put your hands either side of your head.

3 Lift your upper torso toward your knees and over to the right side. At the same time, lift your right leg toward your left shoulder, bending the knee.

4 Hold for a count of 3 then release slowly and return to the start position.

5 Repeat on the other side.

6 Perform 6–8 repetitions.

4

FLOOR EXERCISES

This chapter has a range of basic floor exercises to improve core stability and develop strength and flexibility. They are not meant to be performed as a sequence but rather to act as a guide. Don't worry if you can't complete the full range of movement suggested in each exercise—as you get fitter this will become easier. Some exercises are done on unstable surfaces such as an exercise ball but there are many other types of unstable base equipment you can use if you prefer.

Leg Slide

This exercise will help you learn how to keep your abdominal muscles strong and contracted even when your body is lengthening.

1

3

1 Lie on your back on an exercise mat with your arms by your sides. Keep your knees bent and your pelvis and hips in neutral alignment.

2 Take a deep breath and brace your abdominal muscles by gently drawing your navel in toward your spine.

3 As you breathe out, slowly slide your left foot along the floor, extending your leg until you can no longer keep your abs contracted.

4 Slowly slide the leg back up again to the start position.

5 Perform 3 repetitions and then switch legs.

3

Backstroke

This exercise helps you practice keeping your torso still while the arms move. It also helps to strengthen the lumbar spine.

floor exercises

TIP
Keep your arms wide during this exercise—they shouldn't brush your ears. Keep your body in alignment and the back of the rib cage in contact with the floor throughout.

1 Lie on your back with a pillow under your head and your arms at your sides. Keep your pelvis in neutral and tighten your abdominal muscles.

2 Lift your left arm up to the sky and sweep it back toward the floor behind you, without actually touching the floor. Bring your left arm back up to the center and bring your right arm up to the same point, so that both your arms are straight above your chest, shoulder-width apart.

3 Take your right arm backward and your left arm forward, then bring your right arm back to the center, followed by your left arm.

4 Perform 6–8 repetitions.

Hundreds

This is primarily a breathing exercise designed to strengthen the abdominal region. Make sure you don't arch your lower back.

1 Lie on your back with your knees in the air, directly above your hips, making a 90-degree angle with your lower leg. Keep your arms by your sides.

2 Contract your abdominal muscles to lift your shoulders off the floor. In this position, beat your hands up and down while slowly breathing in and out for a count of 10.

3 Perform 9 repetitions.

1

TIP
If your abs aren't strong enough to do a complete hundred, rest in between exercises. If you feel any strain in the neck, place one hand behind your head to support it and then alternate arms until you've finished.

2

Dog

This classic yoga position strengthens and stretches most of your body. As your flexibility increases you will be able to press your heels into the floor.

floor exercises

57

1 Start on all fours with your hands under your shoulders and your knees under your hips, hip-width apart. Keep your spine in neutral and slowly tighten your abdominal muscles.

2 Curl your toes under, press back into your palms and, bringing the balls of your feet onto the floor, lift your hips toward the ceiling and straighten your legs until you are forming an inverted "V" shape.

YOGA
Many core training exercises come from yoga moves, an ancient form of gentle exercise consisting of body postures and controlled breathing techniques. It's renowned for increasing suppleness and improving mobility.

3 Hold briefly then come down again on all fours.

4 Perform 4 repetitions.

1

2

Basic Curl on an Exercise Ball

This strengthens your rectus abdominis as well as increasing the flexibility of your spine. To make this exercise harder, cross your hands over your chest or behind your head, and bring your feet closer together.

1 Lie on an exercise ball so that your lumbar and midspine are supported by the ball. Place your feet wide apart for stability and your knees bent. Place your arms by your sides so that your hands are either side of your buttocks.

2 Contract your abdominal muscles and curl upward and forward, slowly curling your rib cage toward your pelvis and stretching your arms out in front of you for balance. Hold briefly then slowly release and return to the start position.

3 Perform 6–8 repetitions.

TIP
Keep your movements slow and controlled and do not lift too much—it's the quality of movement that counts.

Reverse Curl

This works your lower abs. You will find that your knees naturally move toward your chest in this exercise, but concentrate on lifting your hips rather than swinging your legs.

2

1 Lie on your back on the floor with your legs raised, knees bent over your hips, and ankles crossed. Place your arms by your sides, palms down.

2 Tighten your abdominal muscles, pulling your navel down toward your spine. Slowly bring your knees toward your chest then lower them by gently tilting your pelvis.

3 Perform 6–8 repetitions.

Oblique Curl

This exercise works your obliques. Try not to pull on your head.

1 Lie on your back with your knees bent and feet flat on the floor, hip-width apart.

2 Cross your left ankle over your right knee. Place your right hand behind your head, elbow bent, and put your left hand on the floor for support.

3 Brace your abs and slowly curl up and over, bringing your right arm toward your left knee, then slowly lower to the start position.

4 Perform 6–8 repetitions then repeat on the other side.

3

Roll-Up with Resistance Band

1

This exercise stretches the spine and builds deep abdominal strength. Make sure you roll down on a soft surface, such as an exercise mat.

1 Sit up straight with your legs extended in front of you, knees bent. Your feet should be parallel and close together. Place the wide part of a resistance band or towel around the balls of your feet and hold the ends of the band. Keep your spine in neutral and tighten your abdominal muscles.

2 Tip your pelvis backward and begin to roll back until your shoulders touch the floor.

2

3 Release your neck, head, and shoulders, letting them down onto the floor.

4 Reverse the movement, rolling back up to a sitting position.

5 Perform 6-8 repetitions.

3

4

Rolling Like a Ball

This exercise improves your balance and the flexibility of your spine and builds strong abdominal muscles.

floor exercises

TIP
Focus on moving from your abdominal muscles rather than letting momentum carry you backward.

1 Sit up with your knees bent and hold your knees with your hands. Pull your abdominal muscles toward your spine to help keep your balance. Tuck your chin into your chest and, staying balanced on your tailbone, lift both feet off the floor.

2 Roll back slowly, bringing your knees closer to your nose until your shoulder blades touch the floor, making sure you do not roll back onto your neck. Then roll forward to the starting position.

3 Perform 3–5 repetitions.

PILATES
This body-conditioning technique focuses on strengthening the core postural muscles to increase your flexibility and mobility.

Basic Bridge

Bridges and planks are static exercises that enable you to assess your core strength by the length of time you are able to hold the positions. They are effective only if you maintain a flat line from your shoulders to your feet.

TIP
Use your hands for balance but don't push yourself up.

1 Lie on your back with your knees bent, feet parallel, hip-width apart, and the heels close to your buttocks. Place your arms by your sides.

2 Tighten your abs and tilt your pelvis as you would in a pelvic tilt.

3 Press your feet down firmly and gently lift your hips, lower and mid back off the floor. Aim to align your hips with your thighs and body. Hold for a count of 10 then release and lower slowly to the floor. Relax.

4 Perform 2 repetitions.

Variation

Bridging using an exercise ball makes your rectus abdominis and external obliques work harder. Lie on your back with your arms by your sides. Place your legs on the ball so that it is resting under your calf muscles. Tighten your abdominal muscles and lift your hips off the floor until your body is diagonal from shoulders to knees. Hold for a count of 10–15 then release and lower slowly to the floor. Relax, then perform 2 repetitions.

FELDENKRAIS METHOD

This is a system of physical re-education designed to improve posture and movement. Simple exercises increase body awareness and increase mobility, and are said to improve both mental and physical health.

Bridge with Leg Extension

Lifting one leg from a stability ball will strengthen the muscles at the back of your buttocks and thighs while increasing balance and control in the stabilizing muscle groups. Do not let your back arch and keep the ball as still as possible throughout.

1 Lie on your back with your arms outstretched. Place your legs on the ball so that it is resting under your calves. Gently tighten your abdominal muscles.

2 Lift your hips up until your body is diagonal from shoulders to knees.

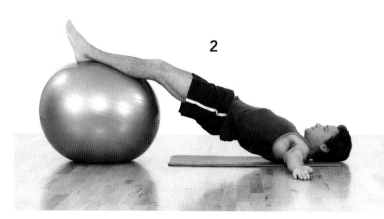

3 With your foot flexed, slowly raise one leg about 12 in (30 cm) off the ball and hold for a count of 10. Slowly release.

4 Repeat using the other leg.

5 Perform 6–8 repetitions.

Side (Lateral) Bridge

It's important not to let your back sag during this exercise and to maintain tension in the abdominal muscles throughout. This is quite challenging and should be attempted only when you can perform basic bridges and planks with ease.

1 Lie on your left side, resting on your left forearm and elbow, your right arm by your side. Keep your knees bent and heels behind you to give you a steady base.

2 Keep your spine in neutral and tighten your abdominal muscles.

3 Lift your hips up toward the ceiling, keeping your torso in line (do not push up with your arms).

4 Hold for 10–15 seconds, then lower and perform 6–8 repetitions.

5 Repeat the exercise, lying on your right side.

2

3

Reverse Bridge on an Exercise Ball

This exercise improves your balance while working your abdominal muscles, lower back, pelvic stabilizers, gluteals, and hamstring muscles. Here you roll into position and roll out again. To increase the difficulty of this exercise you can raise and lower alternate legs once you are in position. The aim is to keep your spine in neutral throughout—do not lift your hips too high.

1 Sit on the ball with your hands by your sides and feet on the floor, hip-width apart.

2 Walk your feet forward, rolling your hips down and lying back on the ball as you do so. Stop when your shoulder blades are on the ball.

3 Lower your head to the ball and lift your hips so that your torso is in a straight line, tightening your abdominal muscles as you do so.

4 Hold for a count of 10.

5 Slowly drop your hips and lift your head off the ball.

6 Walk your feet back, pressing your lower back into the ball as you go, and return to the start position to finish.

Ball Rotation

This exercise should be attempted only when you can perform reverse bridges on an exercise ball with confidence. Just do the exercise once to start with, and then add more repetitions when you can do it easily.

1 Roll into position as if you were doing a reverse bridge. Lie with the ball beneath your shoulders, keep your spine in neutral, and tighten your abdominal muscles.

2 Hold your arms out to the sides. Slowly walk sideways so that the ball moves from one shoulder to the other, then repeat to the other side.

Plank

This exercise works your entire abdominal area as well as your lower back. Use your abdominal muscles to keep your torso stable, not tipped to one side.

TIP

This exercise can be quite challenging. To make it a little easier, just raise your hips and torso away from the floor in step 3 so that your weight is supported by your knees and not your toes.

1 Lie face down on the floor with your elbows under your shoulders and your forearms on the floor.

2 Keep your spine in neutral and tighten your abdominal muscles.

3 Lift your legs and torso away from the floor, keeping your weight supported through your shoulders, forearms, and curled toes

4 Hold for 15–20 seconds or until you begin to lose abdominal tension. Relax and rest for 10 seconds.

5 Perform 3 repetitions.

3

Pushup on a Wobble Board

Try to keep the board stable throughout. You can also use an exercise ball or any other suitable unstable base for this exercise. To increase the difficulty, raise alternate legs with each pushup.

floor exercises

69

TIP
To make this exercise easier, perform the movement with your knees on the floor instead of going up onto your toes.

1 Hold on to the edges of the board, face down, with your legs extended behind you, hip-width apart, and your toes curled under.

2 Keep your spine in neutral and tighten your abdominal muscles.

2

3 Slowly bend your elbows and lower your chest toward the board.

4 Hold briefly then push yourself back up into the starting position.

5 Perform 6–8 repetitions.

3

Swan

This lengthens and strengthens your spine, as well as working your abs. To maintain the tension in your abdominals during this exercise, imagine that you are trying to lift your stomach off the ground.

CAUTION
Consult a doctor before doing this exercise if you have ever had any lower-back problems.

1 Lie on your front with your arms extended in front of you and your legs extended behind.

2 Keep your spine in neutral and tighten your abdominal muscles. You should feel your pubic bone pressing down into the floor.

2

3 Raise your shoulders and feet a few inches off the ground and hold for a count of 10, then release.

4 Perform 2 repetitions.

3

Variation

Performing this move on an exercise ball strengthens and stretches your back. If you can feel any discomfort in your lower back, stop immediately. Lie with the ball under your stomach and pelvis. Plant your curled toes on the floor, hip-width apart, and keep your legs straight. Place your hands on the floor, shoulder-width apart. Tighten your abdominal muscles and lift your head so that there is a long line from your head to your heels. Slowly push your pelvis into the ball as you look up and extend your spine away from the ball. Hold for a count of 5, then release. Perform 3 repetitions.

TIP

Lifting your head helps to lengthen and stretch your spine.

Supine Leg Lift

The importance of this exercise is to hold the legs off the floor with correct spinal alignment and abdominal bracing. Use small ankle weights for extra challenge.

1 Lie on your back with your knees bent and feet on the floor, hip-distance apart.

2 Keep your spine and pelvis in neutral and gently tighten your abdominal muscles.

3 Keeping your knees bent, slowly lift your right leg about 6–8 in (15–20 cm) off the floor and hold it.

4 Now bring your left leg off the floor and bring it adjacent to the right leg.

5 Slowly lower your right leg back to the floor, then the left leg.

6 Perform 6–8 repetitions.

TIP
Each leg movement should be slow and controlled.

Scissors

You will feel a stretch in your
hamstrings as you perform this
exercise but the main aim is to
keep your pelvis, hips, and spine
still and maintain abdominal
tension throughout.

1 Lie on your back with both legs raised, toes
pointing to the ceiling, and knees slightly bent.

2 Keep your spine in neutral and set your
abdominal muscles.

3 Slowly lower your left leg down toward the
floor, still keeping your torso in alignment. From
this position, change the position of your legs in a
scissoring action.

4 Perform 6–8 repetitions on each leg.

2

TIP

To make this exercise more difficult you
can increase the distance over which
the legs are lowered, provided you can
maintain correct alignment.

3

Prone Leg Raise

Leg raises stretch and strengthen your abs, lengthen your lower spine, and strengthen your lower back. Keep your hip bones down on the floor as you do this exercise.

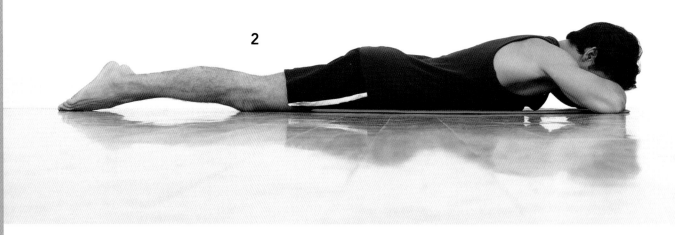

1 Lie on the floor with your arms folded in front of you, your head resting on top of your arms.

2 Keep your pelvis in neutral and gently tighten your abdominal muscles so that your pubic bone is pressing down into the floor. Keep your buttock muscles tight, too.

3 Lift one leg about 6 in (15 cm) off the floor. Hold for a count of 5 then release and raise the other leg.

4 Perform 3–5 repetitions.

Supine Back Extension

This lengthens and strengthens your back as well as working on your core muscles.

1

1 Lie with your middle and lower back on an exercise ball, with your knees bent and your feet hip-width apart and on the floor. Put your hands by the sides of your head for support.

2 Pull your navel in toward your spine to set your abdominal muscles. Let your spine arch backward and relax over the ball and rock gently to and fro for a count of 10.

3 To get out of this position safely, drop your pelvis to the floor and roll off the ball.

2

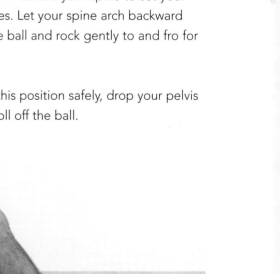

Kneeling Balance

Equipment with an unstable base such as a wobble board or exercise ball is suitable for this exercise. It encourages the core muscles and the muscles surrounding the joints involved to contract effectively so you can keep your balance. You need to do this exercise only once, but as your confidence improves you should try to stay balanced on the ball for longer.

1 Position yourself near a wall and kneel on the board or ball. Place your hands against the wall to help you balance. Sit back on your heels.

2 Tighten your abdominal muscles and lift yourself up so that your spine is in neutral.

3 Take your hands away from the wall to balance unaided. You may find it helps your balance to hold your arms out.

4 Hold for up to 10 seconds and aim to increase the time you can balance.

Superman

This strengthens your back and abdominal muscles and lengthens your spine. Avoid arching your back and keep your movements slow so that you maintain your balance.

1 Position yourself on the floor on all fours. Keep your spine in neutral and set your abdominal muscles.

2 Raise your left arm and your right leg off the floor. Hold this position for up to 10 seconds before returning to the start position.

3 Repeat with the opposite arm and leg.

4 Perform 6–8 repetitions.

Variation

You can do this exercise over an exercise ball but you need to be quite adept at balancing on the ball. Lie face down over an exercise ball so that your fingers and toes are touching the floor. Raise your left arm off the floor and your right leg at the same time.

Single Leg Stretch

This exercise will help you learn to stabilize your abdominals and hips, and will work your entire abdominal area. It will also stretch your back and legs.

floor exercises

TIP
Try to extend your straight leg as much as possible.

1 Lie on your back with your pelvis in neutral. Bend your knees and rest your feet on an exercise ball. Keep your arms by your sides and rest your head on a flat pillow.

2 Set your abs and raise your right leg into the air up to the ceiling, pressing your left leg into the ball.

3 Bring your right leg down and repeat on the left leg.

4 Perform 6–8 repetitions.

Double Leg Stretch

This exercise will make your deep stabilizing muscles work to control the weight and movement of your legs. Along with strengthening your deep abdominal muscles and inner thigh muscles, this exercise aims to build a strong center, which remains stable when you move your arms and legs.

1 Lie on your back with your knees bent and your arms by your sides.

2 Keep your spine in neutral and tighten your abdominal muscles. Pick up the exercise ball between your ankles and squeeze together, pulling your knees toward you.

3 Gently sit up far enough so that you are resting your upper body on your elbows.

4 Straighten your legs out diagonally and hold for a count of 5. Return to the starting position.

5 Perform 6–8 repetitions.

Side Leg Lift

This exercise strengthens your obliques, hips, buttocks, and thighs.

1 Lie on your right side with your legs extended but knees soft rather than locked, toes pointed, and your right arm supported by a cushion or pillow. Rest your left hand on the floor in front of you and support the side of your head with your right hand.

2 Keep your spine in neutral and set your abdominal muscles.

3 Turn your left leg out slightly, then raise it toward the ceiling as far as is comfortable. Hold briefly then slowly release.

4 Perform 6–8 repetitions, then repeat on the other side.

1

3

Side Leg Circles

This exercise tones and strengthens your core muscles as well as the hips, buttocks, and inner thighs.

TIP

Keep your torso in line throughout and don't let it sink forward.

1 Lie on your right side with your head supported by your right hand and your right arm supported by a cushion or pillow. Rest your left hand on the floor in front of you.

2 Bend your right leg in front of you for support.

3 Keep your spine in neutral and set your abdominal muscles.

4 Point your left foot and raise your left leg, raising it as high as feels comfortable. Then draw 5 small clockwise circles with your toes, keeping your abs strong throughout and moving from your hip joint.

5 Reverse the direction and draw 5 small counterclockwise circles, then slowly release.

6 Perform 6–8 repetitions, then repeat on the other side.

5
COOLING DOWN STRETCHES

It is essential to stretch after any exercise routine to release the tension in your muscles and reduce any stiffness or tightness in the joints. These cooling down exercises should be done only when the muscles are warm. Never bounce into position, because you may hurt yourself—feel the stretch but don't overdo it. Keep your stomach muscles braced throughout to protect your lower back.

Seated Spinal Twist

This movement stretches and rotates your abdomen, ribs, and spine and stretches your hip muscles. Make sure you move from your hips up, not from your shoulders down.

1 Sit up straight with your legs out in front of you.

2 Bend your right knee and pull your right foot in to your left buttock. Bend your left knee and place your left foot on your right knee.

3 Gently draw your navel in toward your spine to set your abdominal muscles and slowly rotate to the left. Use your left hand to help keep your body upright. Rotate as far as is comfortable and hold the stretch for at least a count of 15.

4 Release and return to the start position then rearrange your legs so that your right one is on top and rotate to the other side of your body.

TIP
Aim to keep your spine straight throughout and don't arch your back.

1

Knee Hug

This will stretch and release the muscles in your lower back.

1 Lie on your back with your legs in the air and your knees bent. Tighten your abdominal muscles to protect your lower back.

2 Lift your knees to your chest and hold on to your shins.

3 Pull your knees in as tightly as is comfortable and hold for at least 15 seconds. Slowly release, return to the start position, and repeat.

2

3

Lying Twist

Make your movements slowly and evenly, using gravity to push your knee downward. This stretches your back muscles and outer abdominals.

1 Lie on your back with your arms stretched out at shoulder level.

2 Bend your left knee, bringing the heel in, and lift the knee across your body toward the right side.

3 Lower the left knee to the floor, feeling the stretch in your lower back as you twist. Your upper back should stay in contact with the floor.

4 Hold for at least 15 seconds before slowly releasing and returning to the start position.

5 Repeat on the other side of your body.

Cobra

You will feel this stretch in your abdominal muscles and ribs, but avoid pushing yourself too high up off the floor so that there is no risk of straining your back muscles.

CAUTION
Consult a doctor before performing this stretch if you have ever had any lower-back problems.

1

1 Lie face down on the floor with your legs extended and slightly apart, your elbows bent, and your forearms and palms flat on the floor. Keep your spine in neutral and tighten your abdominal muscles.

2 Push your chest and shoulders off the floor so that your upper body is being supported by your elbows and forearms.

3 Hold for at least 15 seconds before slowly releasing and returning to the start position.

4 Repeat once.

2

Cat Stretch

This yoga exercise improves the flexibility of the entire spine.

1 Get into the "box" position (on your hands and knees) with your weight evenly distributed. Your knees should be under your hips and your hands should be under your shoulders.

2 Pull in your abdominal muscles and draw in your navel toward your spine as you arch your lower back upward like a cat.

3 Hold the stretch for 10–15 seconds before slowly releasing.

4 Repeat once.

Variation

Rest your palms on an exercise ball and kneel as far away as possible. Curl your chin into your chest, pull your navel back toward your spine and stretch out your lower back. Hold for a count of 5 then release.

1

2

Child's Pose

This classic yoga position is great
for relaxing your entire back.

1 Get on all fours with your hands under your
shoulders and your knees under your hips.

2 Bring your buttocks back toward your heels,
pulling your navel in against your spine as you do so.
Rest your stomach on your thighs and your head on
the floor. You may find that you cannot sit back on
your heels—in this case, move back only as far as is
comfortable. Take your arms back so that your hands
are close to your feet. Hold the pose for a count of
15 then relax.

Beginners

This workout is ideal if you are just starting out or are looking for a light training session. Choose at least one exercise from each group and vary your exercise routine during the week so you try out each one rather than just sticking to your favorites. Aim to do at least one set of repetitions per exercise, or as indicated, but don't worry if you can manage only a couple to start with. Make sure you warm up properly, following the exercises on pages 28–33, before you start and do the cool-down stretches on pages 84–89 when you have finished.

Standing

Roll Down the Wall (page 36)
Standing on One Leg (page 38)
Standing Leg Lift (page 40)
Lunge (page 42)
Standing Circle (page 44)

Sitting

Seated Forward Spine Stretch (page 45)
Seated Pelvic Tilt (page 47)
Seated Spinal Twist (page 48)

Supine

Leg Slide (page 54)
Backstroke (page 55)
Basic Curl on an Exercise Ball (page 58)
Roll-up with Resistance Band (page 60)
Basic Bridge (pages 62–63)
Single Leg Stretch (page 78)

exercise planners

Prone

Side

GETTING THE MOST FROM YOUR WORKOUT

• Breathe in as you move into position
and breathe out with each effort.

• Keep your spine aligned.

• Pull in your abdominal muscles to protect
your back and to give you a strong core.

• Move slowly and gracefully.

• Stop if you feel any discomfort.

Intermediate

This is a slightly more challenging workout designed for those who are used to exercise. Choose at least one exercise from each group and vary your exercise routine during the week so you try out each one rather than just sticking to your favorites. Make sure you warm up properly, following the exercises on pages 28–33, before you start and do the cool-down stretches on pages 84–89 when you have finished.

GETTING THE MOST FROM YOUR WORKOUT
- Breathe in as you move into position and breathe out with each effort.
- Keep your spine aligned.
- Pull in your abdominal muscles to protect your back and to give you a strong core.
- Move slowly and gracefully.
- Stop if you feel any discomfort.

Standing
Roll Down the Wall (page 36)
Horizontal Balance (page 39)
Standing Leg Lift (page 40)
Lunge (page 42)
Basic Squat (page 43)
Standing Circle (page 44)

Sitting
Seated Forward Spine Stretch (page 45)
Seated Leg Lift (page 46)
Mermaid (page 49)
Seated Reverse Abdominal Curl (page 50)

Supine

Prone

Side

More advanced

This is for experienced exercisers who are looking for more of a challenge. Choose at least one exercise from each group and vary your exercise routine during the week so you try out each one rather than just sticking to your favorites. Increase the amount of sets you do as well. Make sure you warm up properly, following the exercises on pages 28–33, before you start and do the cool-down stretches on pages 84–89 when you have finished.

GETTING THE MOST FROM YOUR WORKOUT
- Breathe in as you move into position and breathe out with each effort.
- Keep your spine aligned.
- Pull in your abdominal muscles to protect your back and to give you a strong core.
- Move slowly and gracefully.
- Stop if you feel any discomfort.

Standing
Standing Forward Bend (page 37)
Horizontal Balance (page 39)
Side Standing Leg Lift (page 41)
Squat with Leg Lift (page 43)

Sitting
Seated Forward Spine Stretch (page 45)
Seated Leg Lift (page 46)
Mermaid (page 49)
Seated Lateral Curl (page 51)

Supine
Hundreds (page 56)
Basic Curl on an Exercise Ball (page 58)
Reverse Curl (page 59)
Oblique Curl (page 59)
Bridge with Leg Extension (page 64)
Ball Rotation (page 67)

Prone

Side

index